—— Little ——

BIG
LAUGHS

JOKE BOOK

FOR KIDS BY KIDS

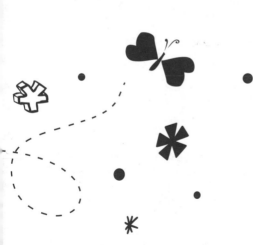

Little Book

BIG
LAUGHS

JOKE BOOK
FOR KIDS BY KIDS

Meg Cadts

UnitedHealthcare
Children's Foundation

Find
Meg Cadts'
Oliver & Hope's
Amusing Adventure
& more at
UHCCF.org.

UnitedHealthcare
Children's Foundation®

ISBN: 978-0-9897937-1-1

Manufactured in the United States of America.
First Printing.

Publisher: UHCCF/Adventure
Author: Meg Cadts and UHCCF
Contact: UnitedHealthcare
                      Children's Foundation

MN017-W400
P.O. Box 41
Minneapolis, MN
55440-0041

1-855-MY-UHCCF (1-855-698-4223)
www.uhccf.org

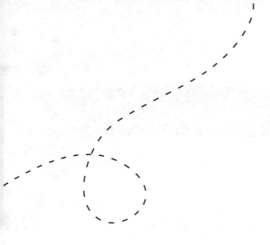

About UnitedHealthcare Children's Foundation

Now, this will make you smile.

Not only does this book deliver hours of good laughs, it also supports a good cause. All the jokes that appear in this book have been shared by the kids through their parents, many of whom have a direct connection to the UnitedHealthcare Children's Foundation.

UHCCF, above all else, is about delivering smiles to children and families that need it most. Since 1999, that mission has included awarding thousands of medical grants, totaling tens of millions of dollars. The sale of this book helps make those grants possible. So remember when you're smiling your way through the following pages, you'll be helping so many more smile along with you.

About UHCCF

The UnitedHealthcare Children's Foundation (UHCCF) is a 501(c)(3) charitable organization that provides medical grants to help children gain access to health-related services not covered, or not fully covered, by their parents' commercial health insurance plan. Families can receive up to $5,000 annually per child ($10,000 lifetime maximum per child), and do not need to have insurance through UnitedHealthcare to be eligible. UHCCF was founded in 1999. Since 2007, UHCCF has awarded more than 6,500 grants valued at over $20M to children and their families across the United States. UHCCF's funding is provided by contributions from individuals, corporations and UnitedHealth Group employees. To apply, donate or learn more, please visit www.UHCCF.org.

PRESENTED TO YOU BY:

TO: _____

From: _____

My Favorite Jokes Are On Pages:

_____

_____

A man went to the doctor because he couldn't stop saying the alphabet. He asked the doctor, "What is wrong with me? Why can't I stop thinking about the alphabet all the time?"

The doctor replied, "Sir, you have A-da-Zs."

Cohen T. | Lexington, KY

Did you hear about the two antennas that got married?

The wedding was really long and a little boring... BUT the reception was fantastic!

Anna F. | Eagan, MN

What does the snail say when riding the turtle?

WHOO HOO.

Anonymous

Why did the cow cross the road?

To go to the MOOOOOvies!

Spencer M. | Savage, MN

Knock Knock.

Who's there?

Cow.

Cow who?

Cows don't who - they moo.

Davis C. | Mansfield, OH

Why do chickens sit on their eggs?

Because chickens don't have chairs!

Jett C. | Gilbert, AZ

Knock Knock.

Who's there?

Who.

Who who?

I didn't know you could speak to owls!

Dale B. | Duluth, MN

Why didn't the skeleton cross the road?

Because he didn't have the guts.

Maxx S. | Burlington, WA

What did the penny say to the dollar?

You don't make any cents.

Juldyz W. | Buffalo, MN

How did the little Scottish Terrier puppy feel when he saw a monster?

Terrier-fied.

Anonymous

Why did the policeman arrest the football player?

Because he was a Steeler.

Hannah E. | Maynard, MA

What do ghosts like for dessert?

I-scream!

Braden B. | Oak Harbor, WA

Why did the chicken cross the playground?

To get to the other slide!

Zoe L. | Red Hook, NY

What is purple, huge and swims in the ocean?

Moby grape.

Anonymous

Why isn't it a good idea to tell a secret in a corn field?

Because the corn have ears!

Sean M. | Easton, PA

UnitedHealthcare
Children's Foundation

Dad: "Son, did you know that you have a banana in your ear?"

Son: "What's that Dad?"

Dad: "I said, you have a banana in your EAR!"

Son: "What's that Dad?"

Dad: "I SAID, YOU HAVE A BANANA IN YOUR EAR!"

Son: "Sorry Dad. I can't hear you. I have a banana in my ear."

William L. | Woods Cross, UT

How does an octopus go into battle?

Fully-armed.

Sarah A. | Chico, CA

What did Mickey say when Minnie asked if he was listening?

I'm all ears!

Ghabriel S. | Neosho, MO

What's the best kind of ship?

Friendship.

James K. | Frisco, TX

Knock Knock.

Who's there?

Snow.

Snow who?

Snow body but me.

Brandon N. | Hermitage, TN

What did the 0 say to the 8?

Nice belt!

Alex R. | Brooklyn Park, MN

Where should you never take a dog?

To a flea market.

Anonymous

Child: Doctor, sometimes I think I've gone invisible.

Doctor: Sorry, I can't see you right now.

Cadence L. | Hermantown, MN

A guy finds a penguin on the beach and goes up to an officer and says "Officer, what should I do with this penguin?"

The officer says "I don't know, take him to the zoo."

The guy says "Yeah, that's a good idea."

The next day the guy and the penguin are hanging out at the beach and the officer sees them and says "Didn't you take him to the zoo?"

And the guy says "Yeah, and he loved it! Next we are going to the movies!"

Vanessa S. | Phoenix, AZ

Why are pirates pirates?

Because they ARRRRR!

Bryce D. | Ramsey, MN

How does a bee brush his hair?

With a honey comb!

Oliver M. | Farmington, MN

What do you call a T-Rex that sets off fireworks?

Dino-mite!

Mylee B. | Oak Harbor, WA

Knock Knock.

Who's there?

Disco.

Disco who?

Disco-nnected.

Meaghan C. | Bloomington, IN

UnitedHealthcare
Children's Foundation

How do you make fruit punch?

Give it boxing lessons!

Glenn B. | Duluth, MN

Why did the dog go swimming?

Because he was a hot dog.

Cobey L. | Roxboro, NC

Why do elephants paint their toenails red?

So they can hide in cherry trees!

Have you ever seen an elephant in a cherry tree?

I didn't think so.

Anthony C. | Robinson, IL

What breaks when you say its name?

Silence.

Jacob A. | Chico, CA

Why did the turtle cross the road?

To get to the "Shell" station.

Caitlyn B. | Deerbrook, WI

Why did the skeleton cross the road?

To get to the body shop.

Dirk H. | Burnsville, MN

Why are giraffe's necks so long?

Because they have smelly feet.

Atikhus B. | Rosenberg, TX

Knock Knock.

Who's there?

Bear.

Bear who?

This joke is UNBEARABLE.

Alayna B. | Kronenwetter, WI

UnitedHealthcare
Children's Foundation

What kind of apple is not an apple?

A pineapple.

Andrew N. | Hermitage, TN

When is it okay to go on red but stop on green?

When you're eating watermelon!

Logan M. | Minnetonka, MN

Knock Knock.

Who's there?

Tank.

Tank who?

Tank you.

Meaghan C. | Bloomington, IN

Why do kindergartners wear red suspenders?

To hold up their smartypants!

Isabel J. | Savage, MN

How does a vampire get across the sea?

In a blood vessel.

Justin W. | Burnsville, MN

Why did Captain Hook cross the road?

To get to the "second-hand" store!

Isaac S. | Santa Rosa, CA

Knock Knock.

Who's there?

Cash.

Cash who?

No thanks, I'd rather have peanuts.

Carson E. | Lynd, MN

UnitedHealthcare Children's Foundation

Have you heard the one about the three holes in the ground?

Well, well, well...

Keaton N. | Duluth, MN

Knock Knock.

Who's there?

Banana.

Banana who?

Knock Knock.

Who's there?

Banana.

Banana who?

Knock Knock.

Who's there?

Orange.

Orange who?

Orange you glad I didn't say banana?

Ansley N. | Middleburg, FL

At a doctor's office registration desk:

Q: When is your birthday?

Patient: July 1st.

Q: What year?

Patient: Every year!

Ronald W. | Cypress, CA

What did one banana say to the other banana?

Nothing, bananas can't talk.

Max R. | Minnetonka, MN

Why can't The Three Bears enter their home?

Because Goldi-locks the doors.

Camden C. | High Point, NC

Why are rabbits so lucky?

They have four rabbit's feet.

Anonymous

Knock Knock.

Who's there?

Panther.

Panther who?

Panther no pants, I'm going swimming!

Lucy D. | Lakeville, MN

What do cows do for fun?

Go to the MOOOOOOO-vies!

Chloe R. | Greenville, SC

**What did the baby corn say
to the mommy corn?**

Where is my pop corn?

Zoe L. | Red Hook, NY

What subject is a witch good at?

Spelling!

Isabel A. | Naperville, IL

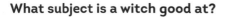

Three copycats were together on a boat. One jumped off. How many were left?

None. They were all copycats.

Carter G. | Maple Grove, MN

Why did the nutty kid throw a bucket of water out the window?

To see a waterfall.

Joshua N. | Eastvale, CA

How come the animals in the zoo can't take tests?

Too many cheetahs!

Thomas M. | Elkridge, MD

What do you get when you cross a porcupine with a balloon?

POP!

Keanna B. | Kronenwetter, WI

What do you call an alligator in a vest?

An investigator!

Anonymous

A math joke:

Teacher: How much is half of 8?

Pupil: Up and down or across?

Teacher: What do you mean?

Pupil: Well, up and down makes a 3 or across the middle leaves a 0!

Sean D. | South Pasadena, FL

Why can't a bicycle stand up by itself?

Because it is two-tired!

Ruben G. | San Diego, CA

What goes oH! oH! oH!?

Santa walking backwards!

Adelyn B. | Orlando, FL

Why did the cowboy get a dachshund?

Someone told him to get-a-long little doggie.

Gavin M. | Roanoke, VA

Why won't dairy cows jump over a barbed wire fence?

Because they would cause udder destruction!

Wade B. | Olathe, KS

What animal needs to wear a wig?

A bald eagle.

Jacob W. | Riverside, CA

What do you call a dinosaur who wears glasses?

Doyouthinkysaurus.

Geb S. | Minneapolis, MN

Why didn't the jack-o'-lantern cross the road?

Because he didn't have any guts.

Madeline Z. | Prior Lake, MN

What do you call it when a puppy kisses you?

A pooch smooch!

Dezirae W. | Harrisburg, SD

I'm going to stand outside. So if anyone asks, I am outstanding.

Ashton K. | Eden Prairie, MN

Why did the dog stay in the shade?

Because it did not want to be a hot dog.

Anonymous

Why did the spider use the computer?

To get to his website!

Andrew E. | Catonsville, MD

Knock Knock.

Who's there?

Interrupting cow!

Interr.... "MOOOOO!" ....upting cow who?

Lexi E. | Ham Lake, MN

What do you call a dinosaur that crashes his car?

A Tyrannasaurus wrecks.

Colton C. | Kansas City, MO

A duck walks into a store and says "Put it on my bill."

Frances S. | Minneapolis, MN

I sure am glad I'm Swedish, because I really do love sweets.

Samuel S. | Maple Grove, MN

What does a cow carry to work every day?

A beef-case.

Brandon W. | Benton, AR

What animal don't you play cards with?

A cheetah!

William D. | Marietta, GA

What do polar bears eat for lunch?

Ice-berg-ers!

Bryson S. | Booneville, MS

Why was the basketball team so cool?

Because they had a lot of fans.

Ben K. | Minneapolis, MN

Knock Knock.

Who's there?

Boo.

Boo who?

Don't cry, it's only a joke!

Joshua R. | Albuquerque, NM

What kind of room has no walls?

A mushroom!

Gabriel L. | St. Louis, MO

What happened when the witch fell off her broom onto the beach?

She turned into a sand-witch.

Juldyz W. | Buffalo, MN

UnitedHealthcare
Children's Foundation

What does a robot frog say?

Rivet, rivet.

Colvin P. | Joplin, MO

How does a pig get to the hospital?

In a ham-bulance!

Kaylynn A. | Fair Oaks, CA

Knock Knock.

Who's there?

Cargo!

Cargo who?

Cargo beep beep!

Michael L. | Two Harbors, MN

Did you hear about the jogger who liked to jog behind cars?

He was exhausted.

What about the jogger who liked to jog in front of cars?

He was tired.

Brendan J. | Minneapolis, MN

What kind of peppers do wolves like to eat?

HOWWWL-a-penos!

AJ G. | Green Bay, WI

What did the water say to the boat?

Nothing, it just waved.

Joe R. | Cottage Grove, MN

What's black, white and red all over?

A penguin with a sunburn.

Scott B. | Jacksonville, FL

How much does a pirate pay to get his ear pierced?

A buck-an-ear!

William D. | Marietta, GA

Knock Knock.

Who's there?

Ghost lion.

Ghost lion who?

RAWR-BOO!

Tierney S. | Coon Rapids, MN

Where does a car go to swim?

A car pool.

Breckyn S. | Newfane, NY

What does a baby computer call his father?

Data!

Anonymous

What did the porcupine say to the cactus?

Is that you mommy?

Jules A. | Temecula, CA

**What do you get if you cross
a Smurf and a cow?**

Blue cheese.

Lauren R. | Maple Grove, MN

**What did one flea say to the other flea as they
were leaving the movie theatre?**

Shall we walk or take a dog tonight?

Anonymous

What kind of animal needs oiling?

A mouse, because it squeaks.

Andrew N. | Hermitage, TN

What time is it when the elephant sits on the fence?

Time to get a new fence!

Sam W. | Eden Prairie, MN

Knock Knock.

Who's there?

Olive.

Olive who?

Olive you!

Avery R. | Pattison, TX

What is the biggest ant in the world?

An eleph-ant.

Phillip S. | Eleva, WI

What goes snap, crackle, squeak?

Mice Krispies.

Shaelie S. | Brainerd, MN

What do you call a fake noodle?

An impasta!

Anonymous

What happens when you throw a blue stone into the Red Sea?

It gets wet!

Michael L. | Two Harbors, MN

Why can't Peter Pan stop flying?

Because he's from Neverland!

William D. | Marietta, GA

How do you keep an elephant from charging?

Take away his credit card!

David S. | Maple Grove, MN

What do you call an elephant in a phone booth?

Stuck!

Jordan B. | Duluth, MN

Knock Knock.

Who's there?

Duck.

Duck who?

Duck duck goose.

Haley L. | Jacksonville, FL

What do you get when you cross a cow and a duck?

Milk and quackers!

Michaell B. | Staten Island, NY

Why do sharks swim in salt water?

Because pepper water makes them sneeze!

Davyn, Liam & Zander H. | Osceola, IN

What are prehistoric monsters called when they sleep?

A dino-snore.

Caitlin H. | Hutchinson, MN

Why can't a nose be 12 inches long?

Then it would be a foot.

Luke E. | Jacksonville, FL

Why were all the football players hot after the game?

Because all the fans left.

Isabelle A. | Montrose, MN

What did the green grape say to the purple grape?

Breathe.

Anonymous

Do you know me?

Yes.

Will you know me in one minute?

Yes.

Will you know me in one hour?

Yes.

Knock knock...

Who's there?

I thought you said you knew me!

Garrett T.　|　Shorewood, MN

Why do seagulls live by the sea?

Because if they lived by the bay, they'd be baygulls! (bagels)

Ansley N.　|　Middleburg, FL

Where do horses live?

In NEIGH-borhoods.

Shaelie S.　|　Brainerd, MN

What is brown and sticky?

A stick.

Emily P. | Savage, MN

Why did the boy bring a ladder to school?

He wanted to go to high school.

Andrew N. | Hermitage, TN

What does a train say when it sneezes?

A-CHOO-CHOO!

Evelyn B. | Robbinsdale, MN

How did the hammer do on his test?

He nailed it!

Jack H. | Pulaski, WI

Why did the mushroom buy everyone pizza?

Because he was a fun-gi.

Cloie G. | Park Rapids, MN

What did the father tomato say to the baby tomato when they were out walking?

Ketchup!

Adam K. | Frisco, TX

What is a cow's favorite animal?

A MOOOOOSE.

Morgan M. | Stokesdale, NC

What fish goes up the river at 100 mph?

A motor pike.

Anonymous

Where do Minnesotans go to eat?

BURRRRRger King!

Jada K. | St. Louis Park, MN

I just flew in from Cleveland...and boy are my arms tired.

Aundrea R. | Little Chute, WI

Knock Knock.

Who's there?

Owls.

Owls who?

Yes, they do!

Elizabeth W. | Duarte, CA

Why aren't grapes ever lonely?

Because they come in bunches.

Anonymous

UnitedHealthcare
Children's Foundation

What is a knight's favorite fish?

A swordfish.

Joshua N. | Eastvale, CA

Why did the witch's baseball team lose?

Because their bats flew away!

Ethan S. | Plymouth, MN

Why should you knock before opening the refrigerator?

Because you may catch the salad dressing!

Anabelle B. | Wilton, NH

Did you know I can jump higher than a building? (Jump in the air)

I can, because buildings can't jump.

Jenna M. | Green Bay, WI

Why can't a T-Rex clap?

Because they are extinct.

Ethan P. | Savage, MN

What's a blue bucket?

A blue bucket.

What's a red bucket?

A blue bucket in disguise.

Colin M. | Minnetonka, MN

Why was the science teacher angry?

He was a mad scientist.

Gabi H. | La Porte, TX

What lies 100 feet in the air?

A dead centipede!

Cooper W. | Indianapolis, IN

Everyone has it and no one can lose it, what is it?

A shadow.

Julia L. | Prior Lake, MN

What's worse than a giraffe with a sore neck?

A centipede with bunions.

Luke E. | Jacksonville, FL

What is always on its way but never arrives?

Tomorrow.

Ryan O. | Oxford, CT

Why do cows wear bells?

Because their horns don't work.

Megan A. | Randleman, NC

What did the right eye say to the left eye?

Don't look down, something smells between us!

Shayni G. | Duluth, MN

What do you call two banana peels?

A pair of slippers!

Keegan T. | Pleasant Hill, CA

What did one stoplight say to the other stoplight?

Don't look! I'm changing...

Amanda B. | Shakopee, MN

What do you call cheese that isn't yours?

Nacho cheese.

Grady H. | Plymouth, MN

What does the cow say when it is sad?

MOO HOO.

Marissa D. | Hudson, NH

Why do teddy bears never eat?

Because they are always stuffed!

Sydney D. | Minnetonka, MN

Why did the pelican leave the restaurant?

Because he had a very large bill.

Colin P. | Guilford, CT

Kid says to the family cat:

Are those your whiskers or do you just have really long nose hairs?

Evan O. | Los Alamitos, CA

Why don't ice fishermen tell jokes?

They are afraid the ice will crack up.

Casey B. | Victoria, MN

Why did the invisible man turn down a job offer?

He just couldn't see himself doing it.

Macy M. | Appleton, WI

Why is it so loud at the barnyard?

Because the cows have horns!

Hailey G. | Rochester, MN

Why did the doctor get mad?

Because he ran out of patients!

Joa G. | South Haven, MN

The fastest dinosaur in the world, goes to town.

What also goes to town and gets there before him?

The road.

Aspen W. | Rothschild, WI

Teacher: Johnny, where's your homework?

Johnny: My dog ate it.

Teacher: Johnny, I've been a teacher for twenty years. Do really expect me to believe that?

Johnny: But, it's true, I swear. I had to force him, but he finally ate it!

Turner W. | Indianapolis, IN

How do you scare a unique frog?

Unique up on it!

Liam L. | Eau Claire, WI

Why did the orange stop rolling?

It ran out of juice!

Braden R. | Port Ewen, NY

What do you call a fish with no eye?

FSSSHHH!

Evan L. | Eau Claire, WI

What does DOG start with?

D.

What does BALL start with?

B.

What does CAR start with?

A key.

Ryan C. | Lexington, KY

What is the sun's pet?

A hot-dog.

Ryann A. | St. Joseph, MO

Student: Teacher, would you be mad at me for something I didn't do?

Teacher: Of course not.

Student: Good, because I didn't do my homework!

Caspar B. | Eden Prairie, MN

Where do sheep go to eat?

To a "BAA-becue"!

Michael T. | New York, NY

How many tickles does it take to make an octopus laugh?

Ten-tickles.

Chloe B. | Phoenix, AZ

How do ducks learn to fly?

They just wing it!

Ellie B.　|　Stilwell, KS

What do you call the two brothers who weren't the first to fly?

The wrong brothers.

Teddy S.　|　St. Louis Park, MN

What do you call a bear with no teeth?

A gummy bear!

Austin N.　|　West Chester, OH

How come the pony couldn't talk?

Because he was a little horse.

Jack B.　|　Shakopee, MN

How do fleas travel?

Itch-hiking!

Riley T. | Minnetonka, MN

Knock Knock.

Who's there?

Doughnut.

Doughnut who?

Do-not come in.

Brad B. | Overland Park, KS

What is a camel's favorite color?

Camel-flauge!

Blake E. | Monongahela, PA

What kind of music did the Pilgrims like?

Plymouth Rock.

Anonymous

Knock Knock.

Who's there?

Noah.

Noah who?

Noah good knock-knock joke?

Jenna M. | Green Bay, WI

Why was the mouse dancing on the peanut butter?

Because it said twist to open.

Tyler B. | Columbus, OH

Knock Knock.

Who's there?

Dwayne.

Dwayne who?

Dwayne the tub, I'm dwowning!

Jenny F. | Proctor, MN

What is a duck's favorite snack?

Quackers.

Jakobie C. | Roanoke, VA

Knock Knock.

Who's there?

Knock Knock.

Who's there?

Knock Knock.

Who's there?

(Joke keeps going and going...)

Kayla M. | Baxter, TN

What did the hand soap say to the lotion that was crying?

Look how moist-your-eyes-are (Moist-ur-i-zer).

Graham V. | Phoenix, AZ

Knock Knock.

Who's there?

Irish.

Irish who?

Irish you a Happy St. Patrick's Day!

Cati L. | Franklin, TN

Why did the dog cross the road?

To get to the barking lot!

CJ C. | Davenport, IA

When does a bee get married?

When he finds his honey!

Carter D. | Woodstock, NY

Why do crocodiles make good cops?

Because they can take a big bite out of crime.

Juldyz W. | Buffalo, MN

Knock Knock.

Who's there?

Little old lady.

Little old lady who?

I didn't know you could yodel.

Ruby G. | Robbinsdale, MN

What do you call it when two cows are talking to each other?

Cow-MOO-ni-cation.

Jesse H. | Garden Grove, CA

Why did the banana go to the hospital?

Because he wasn't peeling well!

Ty'Ana S. | San Antonio, TX

What did Cinderella say to the photographer?

Someday my prints will come in!

Yszabehl S. | Neosho, MO

Where did George Washington keep his armies?

Up his sleevies!

Anonymous

Will you remember me in 7 days?

Yes!

Will you remember me in 14 days?

Yes!

Will you remember me in 30 days?

Yes!

Knock Knock.

Who's there?

You forgot me already...

Sundayah J. | Plano, TX

**A book never written: How To Sneeze.
By: Tish Yoo.**

Nathan Z. | San Diego, CA

UnitedHealthcare
Children's Foundation

What did Sushi A say to Sushi B?

Wasabi! (pronounced like wassup B)

Abby R. | Lafayette, CA

What kind of lollipop is not very smart?

A Dum Dum.

Emily S. | Macungie, PA

Knock Knock.

Who's there?

Cows go!

Cows go who?

No, they don't. They go MOO!

Gabe G. | South Haven, MN

What did one snowman say to the other?

Do you smell carrots?

Ellen H. | New Prague, MN

Why do bananas wear suntan lotion?

Because they peel!

Rachel K. | Phoenix, AZ

What did Mr. and Mrs. Hamburger name their child?

Patty.

Alyssa H. | Menifee, CA

Where do boats go when they are sick?

The dock.

Olivia H. | Bloomington, MN

Which monster is the best dancer?

The Boogie Monster!

Logan B. | Augusta, WI

What did the cowboy say to the cow?

Why don't you M-O-O-O-ve on over?

Ruth Q. | Apple Valley, MN

Mom walks into the room and asks her son "Why do you have super heroes all over the floor?"

Son: "Are you mad? I could give you a cape, and you can be Super MAD and play too."

Orion S. | Naperville, IL

What do you call a snail on a boat?

A snailor.

Madelyn B. | Newnan, GA

Do you know why the moon is full?

Because it ate too much!

Alexa H. | Miami, FL

What did the beef jerky say to the other beef jerky?

Why are you being so jerky?

Alec F. | Avrora, IL

What kind of party does a construction worker like?

A supplies party! (surprise party)

Qvinn S. | Kalamazoo, MI

A student asks his teacher if it's true that tigers and other wild animals won't attack you in the jungle at night if you're carrying a burning torch.

The teacher answers, "Well, young man, it all depends on how quickly you're carrying it."

Daniele M. | Bloomington, MN

UnitedHealthcare Children's Foundation

What is the one flower you can stand on?

The Mayflower!

Jace Y. | Hooksett, NH

There was a man from Leek. Who instead of a nose had a beak. It grew quite absurd, till he looked like a bird. He migrates at the end of next week.

Jacob S. | Merrill, WI

How did the barber win the race?

He knew a short-cut!

Anonymous

A butcher store clerk is 6-feet, 2 inches tall and wears a size 13 shoe. What does he weigh?

Meat.

Madison T. | Snellville, GA

Why did the chicken cross the road two times?

Because he was a double-crosser.

Haley L. | Langhorne, PA

What did the stalactite say to the stalagmite?

I'll meet you in the middle.

Vincent V. | Grantsburg, WI

A man arrived on Friday in a small town. He stayed for two days and left on Friday. How is this possible?

His horse's name is Friday!

Kaiya P. | San Antonio, TX

What's the world's cleanest dog?

A shampoodle.

Anonymous

Why didn't the little pirate get to see the movie?

Because it was rated RRRRRRRR!

Daniel H. | Menifee, CA

Why was the strawberry worried?

Because it was afraid it would be stuck in a jam!

Isabella W. | San Diego, CA

Why did the farmer build a theater on the farm?

So that the cows on the farm can watch a "MOOOO"vie.

Ekadh S. | North Wales, PA

What has a beat, but can't dance?

A heart.

Amelia S. | Saint Paul, MN

What did the glue say to the paper?

I'm stuck on you!

Jayden C. | Oldsmar, FL

Did you hear about the really tall emu that was ignored by the other emus?

He was ostrich-sized.

Gabriel A. | San Antonio, TX

Knock Knock.

Who's there?

Avenue.

Avenue who?

Avenue been missing me?

Calley W. | Schofield, WI

Where do polar bears vote?

The North Pole.

Krystal R. | Hesperia, CA

UnitedHealthcare Children's Foundation

Wanna hear a pizza joke?

Never mind it's too cheesy!

Alex Y. | Westborough, MA

What jumps when it walks and also sits when it stands?

A kangaroo!

Kayla S. | Sunrise, FL

Why did the clown go to the doctor?

He was feeling kinda funny.

Simon K. | Troy, MI

Knock Knock.

Who's there?

I am.

I am who?

You don't know who you are?

John L. | Arden Hills, MN

Who sleeps with their shoes on?

Horses!

Juan C. | Harlingen, TX

Where did the farmer buy his cows?

From a cattle-log! (catalog)

Gavin K. | Plymouth, MN

What do you call a cow in an earthquake?

A milkshake!

Preslie T. | Merrill, WI

Knock Knock.

Who's there?

Banana.

Banana who?

Banana split.

Evan P. | Gaithersburg, MD

What kind of car does Buzz Lightyear drive?

An Infinity and beyond.

AJ P. | Cypress, CA

Why did the elephant get kicked out of the public pool?

He dropped his trunks.

Emily K. | Winter Park, FL

How do you organize a space party?

You planet.

Brian W. | Guilderland, NY

What's more amazing than a talking dog?

A spelling bee.

Anonymous

What time do you have to go to the dentist?

Tooth-hurty!

Henry S. | Sparta, WI

What did the female mushroom say to the male mushroom?

You're a fun-gi.

Timothy V. | Cumming, GA

What dog keeps the best time?

A watch dog.

Emily W. | Merrill, WI

Why aren't Dorothy and Toto in Kansas anymore?

Because they moved to Hollywood.

Anthony W. | Buffalo, MN

Why did the elephant cross the road?

To give the chicken a break.

Ainsley P.　|　Gloucester City, NJ

Knock Knock.

Who's there?

Lettuce.

Lettuce who?

Lettuce in, it's cold out here!

Ava B.　|　Cortlandt Manor, NY

What do you call a rejected scientist?

An astro-not!

Zachary H.　|　Portland, OR

What is a cow's favorite ice cream flavor?

MOO-nilla!

Olivia S.　|　Smyrna, GA

Why did the rubber chicken cross the road?

To get to the rubber band!

Jayden C. | Oldsmar, FL

Knock Knock.

Who's there?

Ding dong.

Ding dong who?

I don't know, you will have to answer the door first!

Marcus N. | Glen Oaks, NY

What do you call a hairy cushion?

A Wookiee-cushion!

Collin W. | Pittsfield, MA

Why don't anteaters get sick?

Because they are full of anty-bodies.

Anonymous

UnitedHealthcare
Children's Foundation

What does the sheep do when he gets dirty?

He takes a BAAA-th.

Elijah T. | San Antonio, TX

What do you call a chimpanzee with a banana in each ear?

Whatever you want, because he can't hear you!

Annabel P. | Mondovi, WI

What do you get when you cross a poodle and a rooster?

A poodle-doodle-doo!

Lila D. | Minneapolis, MN

Where does a cow keep his artwork?

At a MOO-seum.

Jennie Rose F. | Hartford, CT

How does a cow get around town?

On his MOOO-torcycle.

Leah G. | San Antonio, TX

There are two muffins sitting in an oven. One muffin says to the other: "It sure is hot in here."

The other muffin says: "Oh goodness, a talking muffin."

Madison C. | Reseda, CA

What does an astronaut eat for lunch?

Launch meat.

Victoria H. | Lehigh Acres, FL

How does Santa stay so healthy?

He has good elf-care.

Anonymous

Knock Knock.

Who's there?

Keysa.

Keysa who?

Keysa in your pocket.

Ryder F. | Houston, TX

Why did the boy toss the butter out the window?

Because he wanted to see a butterfly!

Cassandra G. | Rancho Cordova, CA

Do you know why elephants paint their toenails different colors?

So they can hide in jelly bean jars.

Have you ever seen an elephant in a jelly bean jar?

See, it works!

Grace L. | Duluth, MN

What is a pirate's favorite vegetable?

An ARRRtichoke.

Madelynn D. | Eastvale, CA

What did sodium say to phosphate when it asked if it liked science?

Na.

Adam P. | Wausau, WI

What is blue and smells like red paint?

Blue paint!

Seren B. | Galena, OH

When does a guinea pig go "MOO"?

When it is learning a new language.

Tony W. | Buffalo, MN

UnitedHealthcare
Children's Foundation

What time does an astronaut eat lunch?

At launch time.

Landon P. | Oviedo, FL

Why did the jelly roll?

Because it saw the apple turnover.

Amelia M. | Plainville, CT

How can you tell if a turkey is eating?

You can hear it GOBBLE-ing!

Mary P. | Oakdale, CA

What fish can perform operations?

A sturgeon.

Anonymous

Why did the monkey climb the tree?

To get a banana, silly!

Loftyn A. | Elk Mound, WI

What do you call a frog driving a truck?

A toad truck.

Zahn O. | Dallas, TX

Why did the man cross the road?

Because he was Super-Glued to the chicken.

Owen S. | Dresser, WI

What did the buffalo say to his son when he dropped him off at school?

Bison.

Elizabeth A. | New Brighton, MN

Try saying this five times fast:

Pretty purple pansies produce pretty petals.

Tanner S. | Cape Coral, FL

Knock Knock.

Who's there?

Luke.

Luke who?

Luke through the peep hole and I'll tell you.

Branson B. | South Windsor, CT

What did the wall say to the other wall?

Meet you at the corner.

Colin M. | San Francisco, CA

Why do ghosts ride elevators?

Because it lifts their spirits!

Brookelynn B. | Augusta, WI

How do pigs send secret messages?

With invisible oink.

Anonymous

Knock Knock.

Who's there?

You.

You who?

Are you calling me?

Addison T. | Pleasant Hill, CA

What do you call a pig in karate?

Porkchop!

Manny C. | Weslaco, TX

Where are sports shirts made?

New Jersey!

Hannah H. | International Falls, MN

Knock Knock.

Who's there?

Ach.

Ach who?

Bless you.

Angel A. | Whittier, CA

Try saying this five times fast:

Tanner took two tan turtles Tuesday to tease turkeys twisting taffy treats.

Tanner S. | Cape Coral, FL

Why is a piano so hard to open?

Because the keys are on the inside!

Ellan S. | Booneville, MS

What do you call a happy farmer?

A Jolly Rancher.

Brenton P. | Helotes, TX

Knock Knock.

Who's there?

Dishes.

Dishes who?

Dishes me, who are you?

Andrew J. | Delmar, DE

What kind of wood barks?

Dogwood.

Vincent V. | Grantsburg, WI

Why do hummingbirds hum?

Because they forgot the lyrics of the song.

Melaya D. | Eastvale, CA

What did the flower say to the bumblebee?

Buzz off!

Tony W. | Buffalo, MN

What is as big as an elephant and weighs nothing?

An elephant's shadow.

Caitlyn R. | Andover, CT

What do you call a pig who just took a bath?

Squeaky clean!

Molly M. | Omaha, NE

What is a ghost's favorite thing to eat?

BOOberries.

Gabrielle P. | Chippewa Falls, WI

Why don't they play football in Africa?

Because there are so many cheetahs.

Alyssa M. | Republic, MO

What's a plumber's favorite vegetable?

A leek.

Eli Lee B. | Winchester, KY

Why did the mommy grape have to go to the spa?

Because she needed a break from raisin' her bunch of kids.

Anonymous

What do you call a class in a tree?

High school.

Jack E. | Chanhassen, MN

Why are basketball players sloppy eaters?

Because they are always dribbling!

Mackenzie W. | Riverside, CA

Why don't scarecrows tell jokes?

Because they're usually too corny!

Katie M. | Tampa, FL

What did the back of the quarter say to the front?

I am a quarter-back.

Nicholas S. | Eden Prairie, MN

What is red, black, red, black, red, black, red, black, etc.?

A sunburned zebra.

Sam V. | De Pere, WI

What is a cow's favorite movie?

Sound of MOOsic.

Sarah A. | Chico, CA

Grandma asked her granddaughter how she liked school.

The granddaughter said "CLOSED!"

Kaitlyn S. | Macomb Township, MI

Why couldn't the pirates play cards?

They were sitting on the deck!

Nora M. | Hatley, WI

What kind of music do mummies like?

Wrap!

Anonymous

UnitedHealthcare
Children's Foundation

What did the cow call his guacamole?

Guaca-MOOOOO-le.

Shiloh G. | Pembroke Pines, FL

What did the pencil say to the ruler?

You rule!

Dezi W. | Buffalo, MN

What's a volcano's favorite food?

Lava cake.

Randy D. | Pittsburgh, PA

Knock Knock.

Who's there?

Kook!

Kook who?

Who are you calling a kookoo?

Melora S. | Sarasota, FL

What did the ear of corn say when all his clothes fell off?

Ah, shucks!

Joey Q. | Plymouth, MI

What dog can jump higher than a building?

Any dog, buildings can't jump.

Milana K. | Portland, CT

Why can't you say a joke while standing on ice?

Because it might crack up!

Jacob A. | Merrill, WI

What did the dog say when he sat on the sandpaper?

RUFF.

Luke E. | Illinois City, IL

Knock Knock.

Who's there?

Banana.

Banana who?

Gee, I could eat a banana right now, do you have one?

Richard D. | Dallas, TX

What did the salt say to the pepper?

Seasoning's Greetings!

Kaya W. | La Crosse, WI

How do you catch a school of fish?

With a bookworm.

Amberlynn P. | Bridgeport, CT

Knock Knock.

Who's there?

Bacon!

Bacon who?

Bacon a cake for your birthday!

Christian R. | Manchester, NH

Why did the pig cross the road?

To give the chicken a piggyback ride.

Jacob A. | Chico, CA

What did the cat say about the cake?

It's PURRRRRRfect!

Bryson A. | Greensboro, NC

What is a frog's favorite year?

Leap year!

Aiden B. | Augusta, WI

What do you get when you cross a goldfish and an elephant?

Swim trunks!

Kylie H. | International Falls, MN

What did the kitten say when it bumped its head?

Me-OWW!

Dezi W. | Buffalo, MN

How does the ocean say hello?

With a great big wave!

Jack C. | Cromwell, CT

Why didn't Cinderella make the basketball team?

She ran away from the ball.

Anonymous

Knock Knock.

Who's there?

Nobel.

Nobel who?

No bell, that's why I knocked!

Anonymous

What do you call a pig that is grounded?

A groundhog.

Rithika R.　|　Woodbury, MN

What is a dog's favorite dessert?

Pup-cakes!

Mylee B.　|　Oak Harbor, WA

What color socks do bears wear?

They don't wear socks, they have bear feet.

Catalina K.　|　Portland, CT

UnitedHealthcare Children's Foundation

What do baseball players on third base like to sing?

There's no place like home.

Antonio P. | Bridgeport, CT

Knock Knock.

Who's there?

Pizza.

Pizza who?

Pete's a really nice guy!

Christopher R. | Toledo, OH

What did the lamp say to the other lamp?

It's going to be a BRIGHT day!

Colin M. | San Francisco, CA

Why did silly Sarah take sugar to bed?

So she would have sweet dreams.

Bailey C. | Trumbull, CT

Where did the sheep get his haircut?

At the BAH-BAH shop.

Jessica S. | Branford, CT

Knock Knock.

Who's there?

Hatch.

Hatch who?

Ha ha, made you sneeze.

Addie S. | New Hope, MN

Knock Knock.

Who's there?

Theodore.

Theodore who?

Open Theodore, and let me in!

Theodore V. | De Pere, WI

What kind of mouse walks on two legs?

Mickey Mouse.

What kind of duck walks on two legs?

All ducks walk on two legs.

Kane B. | Chico, CA

What flower gets tan a lot?

A sunflower.

Vincent V. | Grantsburg, WI

How much money does a skunk have?

One scent.

Jacob W. | Riverside, CA

What did the farmer say to the horse?

What's with the long face?

Dezi W. | Buffalo, MN

What do you get when you cross a Cocker Spaniel, a rooster and a poodle?

A cockerpoodledoo!

Rvsne N. | Edina, MN

The little spider asked, "Mommy, where does silk come from?"

The Mommy spider replied, "Look it up on the web, dear!"

Tyler R. | Mastic Beach, NY

What did the duck say when he went to the drugstore to buy Chapstick?

Just put it on my bill.

Maya F. | Kingwood, TX

What did the tie say to the hat?

You go on ahead and I'll hang around!

Annabel P. | Mondovi, WI

UnitedHealthcare
Children's Foundation

Pete and Repeat were in a boat.

Pete fell out.

Who was left?

Repeat.

Pete and Repeat were in a boat.

Pete fell out.

Who was left?

Repeat.

Milana K. | Portland, CT

Knock Knock.

Who's there?

Apple.

Apple who?

Apple pie!

Caden K. | Wausau, WI

Why did the bird cross the kitchen?

To-eat, to-eat (pronounced tweet, tweet).

Izabel C. | Latham, NY

What did one owl say to the other owl?

Owl always be your friend!

Brookelynn B. | Augusta, WI

There is a BLUE house, a RED house and a GREEN house.

What is the BLUE house made of?

Blue bricks.

What is the RED house made of?

Red bricks.

What is the GREEN house made of?

Glass!

Jeremy N. | Chino Valley, AZ

What is the difference between a teacher and a train?

A teacher says "spit your gum out" and a train says "choo, choo, choo."

Blake D. | Lakeville, MN

UnitedHealthcare
Children's Foundation

What is the first thing a dolphin learns in school?

Her A-B-Seas!

Bailey C. | Trumbull, CT

Who is Minecraft's favorite football team?

The "Seattle Sea Blocks."

Spencer B. | Corrales, NM

What is a ninja's favorite drink?

WAAAA-TAAAA!

Nolan M. | Pelham, NH

What did the salt say to the pepper?

What's shaking, hot stuff?

Jada D. | Wittenberg, WI

What's a boxer's favorite drink?

Punch!

Natalia L. | Miami, FL

What swan plays good music?

A Trumpeter Swan.

Vincent V. | Grantsburg, WI

What did the frog order at McDonald's?

French Flies and Diet Croak.

Emerson F. | Prior Lake, MN

Why couldn't the skeleton dance?

Because he has no "body" to dance with!

Olivia S. | Smyrna, GA

What is hairy and coughs?

A coconut with a cold!

Elijah T. | San Francisco, CA

Why does a chicken coupe have only 2 doors?

Because if it had 4 doors it would be a chicken sedan!

Destiny D. | Hialeah, FL

How do you get Pikachu on the bus?

You Pokémon!

Declan R. | Niagara Falls, NY

Why was the baby ant confused?

Because all of his uncles were ants!

Westley P. | Mondovi, WI

What do you get from a pampered cow?

Spoiled milk!

Cassidy O. | St. Louis, MO

How do you fix a broken pizza?

With tomato paste.

Joseph M. | Bloomfield, NJ

What do you call a cat who is in the freezer for a long time?

The coolest cat in town!

Caden B. | Indianapolis, IN

What did the skyscraper say to the other skyscraper?

High there!

Colin M. | San Francisco, CA

What is 1 infinity plus 1 infinity?

2 infinity and beyond!

Brvin B. | Tempe, AZ

What is black and white, black and white, black and white?

A penguin rolling down a hill!

Megan A. | Randleman, NC

Doctor, Doctor! I feel like a spoon! Well, sit still and don't stir!

Brianna M. | Mondovi, WI

What do you call a boomerang that doesn't return after you throw it?

A stick.

Joe K. | Minneapolis, MN

What do you call a person who makes a bull go to sleep?

A bull-dozer.

Vincent V. | Grantsburg, WI

Why didn't the skeleton have a job?

Because he had lazy bones!

Cimone N. | Saint Charles, MO

What did the tree say to the other tree?

Leaf me alone!

Colin M. | San Francisco, CA

What do you get when you cross a turtle and a porcupine?

A slow-poke!

Anonymous

What's a caveman's favorite meal?

Club sandwich.

Jesse B. | Islandia, NY

Why did the dog sit on the watch?

He wanted to be a watchdog.

Maxwell C. | Clinton, NJ

Knock Knock.

Who's there?

Izabel.

Izabel who?

Is a bell (Izabel) really necessary on a bicycle?

Izabel C. | Latham, NY

What is a cat's favorite kind of fish?

Catfish.

Alayna B. | Kronenwetter, WI

What type of trucks do monsters like to drive?

Monster trucks.

Aaron S. | Sophia, NC

What do you get when you cross a sheep with a speckled chicken?

A spotted sweater!

Kylie H. | International Falls, MN

Two peanuts were walking in the park.

One was a-salted.

Anonymous

What is the biggest mouse in the world?

A Hippopota-mouse!

Hayden S. | Booneville, MS

Knock Knock.

Who's there?

Ivan.

Ivan who?

I-van-to suck your blood!

Olivia S. | Phoenix, AZ

What does a clock do when he gets hungry?

He goes back for seconds!

Natalie T. | Grandview, MO

Where does a pencil live?

Pennsylvania!

Max T. | Rochester, MN

What is a cat's way of keeping law and order?

Claw enforcement.

Haley L. | Jacksonville, FL

How does a bee get to school?

A school BUZZZZZ.

Savannah H. | Plainfield, IN

Where do operators learn their numbers?

Call-ege.

Olivia E. | Willard, MO

When does Friday come before Thursday?

In the dictionary.

Zoria D. | High Point, NC

How do you keep a dog from barking in your front yard?

You put it in your backyard.

Anonymous

What has four legs and can't walk?

A chair.

Avery K. | Appleton, WI

Why is a soccer ball sad?

Because it keeps getting kicked.

Hailie H. | Apple Valley, MN

Why did King Kong climb the Empire State Building?

Because he couldn't fit in the elevator!

Alexis B. | Anaheim, CA

What happened when the T-Rex took the train home?

He had to bring it back!

Pixi R. | San Antonio, TX

What is a cow's favorite game?

MOO-sical chairs.

Evelyn C. | Clinton, NJ

A boy asks his father, "Dad, are bugs good to eat?"

Dad: "That's disgusting, don't talk about things like that over dinner."

After dinner the father asks, "Now, son, what did you want to ask me?"

Son: "Oh, nothing, there was a bug in your soup, but now it's gone."

Anonymous

Why did the bank robber take a shower?

He wanted to make a "clean" getaway.

Jake D. | Merrill, WI

UnitedHealthcare Children's Foundation

What's a cat's favorite color?

PURRR-ple.

Hunter H. | Wildwood, MO

Why is the skeleton afraid to climb the mountain?

Because he has no guts!

William D. | Marietta, GA

Two cows in a field:

Cow #1: MOO.

Cow #2: Dude, how do you do that?

Cow #1: Do what?

Cow #2: Read my mind.

Taylor E. | Laguna Niguel, CA

When do ducks wake up?

At the quack of dawn.

MacKinley M. | Shelby Township, MI

Knock Knock.

Who's there?

Figs.

Figs who?

Figs the doorbell, because it's broken!

Annabel P. | Mondovi, WI

If 6 kids and 2 dogs are under an umbrella, why don't they get wet?

Because it's not raining.

Matthew N. | Eastvale, CA

What do you get when you cross a centipede with a parrot?

A walkie-talkie!

Zane R. | Knoxville, TN

UnitedHealthcare Children's Foundation

Why did the boy take a pencil to bed?

To draw the curtains.

Avery K. | Appleton, WI

How do you know that ice is laughing?

It cracks up.

David L. | Durham, NC

How do turtles make phone calls?

On their shell phones!

Ayden R. | Chico, CA

Have you ever seen a catfish?

Yes.

Not possible, how would he hold the rod and reel?

Anonymous

What is the best thing to put in a cake?

Your teeth.

Sophia C. | Isleton, CA

When does the alphabet only have 24 letters?

When U and I aren't there!

Cassidy Q. | St. Louis, MO

Why don't you iron a four leaf clover?

You'd be pressing your luck.

Joyce G. | Omaha, NE

Try saying this five times fast:

Irish Wristwatch.

Riley F. | Union, CT

Why do stop lights use light bulbs?

Because they don't have flash lights!

Jett C. | Gilbert, AZ

Why can't dogs work the DVD remote?

Because all they can hit is the "paws" button!

Tabitha G. | O'Fallon, MO

What does a space frog say?

ORBIT, ORBIT.

Will S. | Anthem, AZ

How did the farmer fix his jeans?

With a cabbage patch.

Zachary B. | Foothill Ranch, CA

What do you call a group of rabbits hopping backwards?

A receding hare line.

Anonymous

Knock Knock.

Who's there?

Butter.

Butter who?

Butter open the door, it's cold outside!

Hayden N. | Keller, TX

Why was the man who was building the puzzle proud when he finished it in one hour?

Because on the box it said 3 years and up!

Ryder M. | Scotts Valley, CA

Can a kangaroo jump farther than the Great Wall of China?

Yes, because the Great Wall of China cannot jump.

Sydney C. | Newton, MA

How do you find King Arthur in the dark?

With a knight light.

Joshua N. | Eastvale, CA

What position does a ghost play in soccer?

Ghoulie!

Braden B. | Oak Harbor, WA

Why did Mickey Mouse go into space?

To find Pluto!

Chloe B. | Fleming Island, FL

What happens when the sky gets a cold?

It coughs up a storm!

Zaira A. | Carlsbad, CA

How did the frog get over the wall?

With a tadpole.

Stokes D. | Franklin, TN

Why didn't the turkey go to Thanksgiving?

Because he was already stuffed!

Brianna M. | Mondovi, WI

Why do strings never win?

Because they can only tie.

Rhema S. | Springfield, MO

What does an octopus wear in the winter?

A coat of arms.

Phillip S. | Eleva, WI

Woman: "Doctor, Doctor! My little boy has just swallowed a roll of film!"

Doctor: "Hmm. Let's hope nothing develops."

Sofie S. | San Diego, CA

When does a teacher carry birdseed?

When there is a parrot-teacher conference.

Anonymous

What has four wheels and flies?

A garbage truck.

Jesse P. | Crossville, TN

Knock Knock.

Who's there?

Silly.

Silly who?

Silly hotdog.

Brady Q. | Deerfield, NY

What is a baby's favorite reptile?

A rattle-snake.

Gabi H. | La Porte, TX

Where does a hamster go for spring break?

Hamsterdam.

Anonymous

Why does a bee always have sticky hair?

Because it uses a honey comb!

Becca P. | Mondovi, WI

UnitedHealthcare Children's Foundation

Why did the cupcake go to school to learn how to work in a restaurant?

It wanted to be a Hostess!

Chloe B. | Fleming Island, FL

What kind of viper loves water?

A windshield viper.

Henry S. | Las Vegas, NV

What game does the cat like to play with the mouse?

Catch!

Theodora G. | Lodi, NJ

What do you call macaroni that you are allergic to?

Macaroni and sneeze!

Devlin G. | Castleton on Hudson, NY

Why can't a leopard hide?

Because he's always "spotted".

Anonymous

Why couldn't Batman go fishing?

Because Robin ate all the worms.

Carter K. | Appleton, WI

How many jelly beans can you put in an empty jar?

None, because it won't be empty any more.

Nicholas S. | Eden Prairie, MN

What did the volcano say to the other volcano?

I lava you!

Jenna N. | Eastvale, CA

What did the ghost say to his girlfriend?

You're BOOOO-tiful!

Kylie H. | Cypress, CA

Knock Knock.

Who's there?

Tank.

Tank who?

You're welcome!

Dillon L. | North Las Vegas, NV

What is a tree's favorite drink?

Root beer!

Ellan S. | Booneville, MS

How does a witch tell time?

With a witch-watch!

Mylee B. | Oak Harbor, WA

Why was the banana pulled over?

He was seen peeling out of the parking lot.

Ysabel D. | Chico, CA

A man went into his doctor's office complaining of back pain.

The doctor asked him. "When did your back start hurting?"

The man answered "Oh, about a week back."

Matthew M. | Deer Park, TX

Why did the girl eat her homework?

Because the teacher told her it was a piece of cake.

Mackenzie W. | Riverside, CA

How does an astronaut read in bed?

He turns on a sate-light.

Bailey C. | Trumbull, CT

Why was the horse so happy?

He was in a stable environment.

Jonathan B. | Piscataway, NJ

Why was the birthday cake as hard as a rock?

Because it was a marble cake.

Anonymous

What did the pickle say to the other pickle who went inside the pickle jar to find a perfect pickle?

Picky!

Isabella S. | Danbury, CT

What did the rabbit give his bride?

24-carrot diamond.

Nick D. | Franklin, TN

What did Santa give Rudolph for his upset stomach?

Elk-a-Seltzer.

Asa D. | Bay Shore, NY

Why was the broom late for school?

Because it over swept.

Natalie K. | Colorado Springs, CO

Why did the girl sleep with a ruler?

To measure how long she slept!

Avery K. | Appleton, WI

How do you make seven an even number?

Take away the "S".

Milana K. | Portland, CT

During a health day at school, a boy asked his brother a question.

Brother 1: "What is your favorite nut? Cashews, pecans, walnuts?"

Brother 2: "Well... Donut!"

Anika B. | Chelmsford, MA

What does a clam do on his birthday?

He shell-a-brates.

Anonymous

Why did the old lady want wheels on her rocking chair?

So she could Rock and Roll.

Mackenzie W. | Riverside, CA

What did the egg say to the frying pan?

You crack me up.

Shaelie S. | Brainerd, MN

What do you call two trees in a river?

Swimming trunks!

Hailey G. | Rochester, MN

What do you call a pup that is cold?

A pupsicle.

Rhema S. | Springfield, MO

What do you call a thief that steals only meat?

A Hamburglar!

Nicholas V. | Greensboro, NC

Why did the spider cross the road?

To get to the other website!

Catherine W. | Duarte, CA

UnitedHealthcare Children's Foundation

The man ordered soup and then the waiter came by and said, "Is there anything wrong with your soup?"

The man replied, "Yes."

The waiter asked, "Is it too cold or too hot?"

The man said, "Just try it." The waiter said, "Ok, where is the spoon?"

The man replied, "A-ha!"

Sydney D. | Minnetonka, MN

What do you give a sick lemon?

Lemon-aid.

Anonymous

Knock Knock.

Who's there?

Tuba.

Tuba who?

Tube a toothpaste.

Jackson F. | Newark, OH

What kind of car does a cat drive?

A Cat-illac!

Sophie K. | International Falls, MN

Who do you call for a vampire whose car broke down?

A cab.

Ben W. | Parsippany, NJ

Why did the picture go to jail?

Because it was framed.

Tyler A. | Las Vegas, NV

Why did the banana cross the road?

Because it wanted to split!

Lucas H. | Westminster, CA

UnitedHealthcare Children's Foundation

Why did the cow jump over the moon?

So it could get some over time.

Joshua R. | Cypress, CA

What candy do you eat on the playground?

Recess Pieces.

Anonymous

What goes up when the rain comes down?

An umbrella.

Blake O. | Manchester, CT

What is a mountain's favorite kind of candy?

Sno-Caps!

Emily V. | Castleton, NY

What bird is always out of breath?

A Puffin.

Andrea S. | Eleva, WI

When does a car greet you?

When driving on the Hi-way!

Sathvik N. | Dallas, TX

Why did the whale cross the ocean?

To get to the other tide!

Nicholas V. | Greensboro, NC

How do you get a baby astronaut to sleep?

You rocket!

Hayden S. | Booneville, MS

What's white, has a horn and gives out milk?

A dairy truck.

Anonymous

Why did the crab not share his toys?

Because he was shellfish!

Katelyn D. | Anaheim, CA

What is it called when two snowmen are talking?

Snow-cializing!

Morgan S. | Simpsonville, SC

Why was the crab crabby when he woke up?

The sea snore kept him up all night.

Jacob K. | Illinois City, IL

Why did the police arrest the turkey?

Because they suspected him of fowl play.

Anonymous

What did the pumpkin call his date?

His gourd-friend.

Kaya E. | Westminster, MA

What's the difference between a TV and a newspaper?

Have you ever tried swatting a fly with a TV?

Joseph D. | Kerhonkson, NY

How does a fish go on the web?

In-her-net.

Waylon G. | Park Rapids, MN

Why did the elephant go on vacation?

He already had packed his trunk.

Megan B. | De Pere, WI

Where do strawberries play their saxophones?

At "jam" sessions!

Jacob W. | Riverside, CA

Why did the clock get sick?

It was run down.

Richard H. | Woodstock, NY

Why did the girl smear peanut butter on the road?

To go with the traffic jam!

Madison L. | Grayling, MI

What key has legs and can't open doors?

A turkey.

Anonymous

Where do spiders get their music?

On the web.

Jadyn R. | Illinois City, IL

What kind of coat do you put on wet?

A coat of paint!

Katelyn D. | Anaheim, CA

Hey waiter, will my pizza be long?

No sir, it will be round.

Madison S. | Rochester, MN

UnitedHealthcare Children's Foundation

Why did the elephant paint the bottom of its feet yellow?

So he could hide upside down in custard.

Did you ever find an elephant in custard?

No, it must work then!

Nicole P. | Scottsdale, AZ

Why was the ghost a bad liar?

You could see right through him!

Samson G. | St. Louis, MO

What is a hamburger's favorite day of the week?

French fry-day.

Bailey C. | Trumbull, CT

Would you like to know why my best friend is a squirrel?

He only likes me because I'm "nuts."

Kayla M. | Baxter, TN

Knock Knock.

Who's there?

Orange.

Orange who?

Orange you glad I'm not a monster?

Kaleb S. | Macon, GA

Where do cows get their medicine?

From the farm-acy!

Mackenzie W. | Riverside, CA

When is a birthday cake like a golf ball?

When it is sliced.

Anonymous

How do you make a tissue dance?

Put a little boogie in it.

Julian J. | Oakdale, MN

UnitedHealthcare Children's Foundation

Knock Knock.

Who's there?

Beets.

Beets who?

Beets me, I thought you'd know.

Derek R. | Old Bridge, NJ

You know when you see a flock of birds flying in the sky, and one side of the "V" formation is longer than the other side. Do you know why that is?

It's because there are more birds on the longer side.

Nicholas P. | Minneapolis, MN

What subject are snakes good at?

HISSS-tory!

Becca P. | Mondovi, WI

A little girl goes to visit her doctor. She has a carrot in her left ear, a tomato in her right ear and a banana in her nose.

"What's the matter with me?" she asks her doctor.

The doctor replies, "My dear girl, you're not eating properly."

Daniele M. | Bloomington, MN

What's an elf's favorite kind of cake?

Short-cake.

Anonymous

What did the teacher seagull say to her class?

Good morning boys and gulls!

Morgan S. | Simpsonville, SC

What do you call a cow without any milk?

A Milk Dud.

Emma D. | Chico, CA

Have you seen the tomato website?

I will ketchup with it later.

Jeremiah K. | Illinois City, IL

What does a rock do when it listens to music?

It Rocks and Rolls.

Alex K. | Fridley, MN

What is white, has four long ears, whiskers and sixteen wheels?

Two rabbits on Rollerblades!

Camden C. | High Point, NC

What is loud and sounds like 'apple'?

APPLE! (Say it really loud)

Keely M. | Minneapolis, MN

What do you get when you combine ten female pigs with ten male deer?

Twenty sowz-and-bucks.

Rhema S. | Springfield, MO

What kind of car does Mickey Mouse's wife drive?

A Minnie van.

Jacob W. | Riverside, CA

Try saying this five times fast:

A skunk sat on a stump. The stump thought the skunk stunk. The skunk thought the stump stunk. What stunk? The skunk or the stump?

Braden B. | Oak Harbor, WA

What do you get if you divide the circumference of a pumpkin by its diameter?

Pumpkin pi.

Anonymous

Knock Knock.

Who's there?

Half a cake.

Half a cake who?

Have a cake and eat it too!

Sawyer G. | St. Louis, MO

What did the math book say to the story book?

Boy, do I have problems!

Jazmine T. | San Antonio, TX

What does a river eat?

Anything that falls into its mouth.

Vincent V. | Grantsburg, WI

What do you call Chewbacca when he has chocolate stuck in his hair?

A Chocolate Chip Wookiee!

Ghabriel S. | Neosho, MO

Why did the octopus cross the road?

To get a pen for its ink!

Ryan M. | Marlborough, CT

What did the boy fish say to the girl fish?

Can I sea-mail you sometime?

Greylyn Z. | Tucson, AZ

What happens twice every moment but only once in a minute?

The letter "M."

Abby S. | Plymouth, MN

How do you turn soup into gold?

Add 24 carrots!

Garrison C. | Richardson, TX

How did the soup lose his job?

He got canned.

Alex Q. | Lyndon, IL

Why did the bird go online?

He wanted to tweet.

Timothy L. | Towaco, NJ

What is the wettest animal in the world?

A reindeer!

Gvoste N. | Edina, MN

How did Darth Vader know what Luke got him for Christmas?

He felt his presence (presents)!

Braden B. | Oak Harbor, WA

The more I dry the wetter I get...what am I?

A towel!

Breda C. | Plymouth, MN

What do you get when an elephant sits on your couch?

A new couch.

Carson C. | High Point, NC

Knock Knock.

Who's there?

Ben.

Ben who?

Ben knocking for 10 minutes.

Nora M. | Merrill, WI

UnitedHealthcare Children's Foundation

Which flower talks the most?

Tulips, of course, because they have two lips!

Madison L. | Grayling, MI

How much did the hipster weigh?

An Instagram.

Hallie K. | Prior Lake, MN

Try saying this five times fast:

Tommy took Toby to town to tinker test toys.

Tanner S. | Cape Coral, FL

I have a joke about butter, but I won't tell you because you might spread it around.

Wyatt K. | Las Vegas, NV

What do you get when you cross a music composer and a rotten pumpkin?

A decomposer.

Julia N. | Eden Prairie, MN

Knock Knock.

Who's there?

Goliath.

Goliath who?

Goliath down, you look tired.

Avndrea R. | Little Chute, WI

Knock Knock.

Who's there?

Love.

Love who?

I love you.

Alayna B. | Kronenwetter, WI

UnitedHealthcare Children's Foundation

What kind of dog does a vampire have?

A Bloodhound.

Anonymous

What does a pirate like to do on the weekend?

YARRRRD work!

William D. | Marietta, GA

What do elves learn in school?

The elf-abet.

Andrew N. | Hermitage, TN

What's a race car driver's favorite food?

Fast food.

Matthew N. | Eastvale, CA

What does a slice of toast wear to bed?

Jammies.

Bailey C. | Trumbull, CT

How does a skunk call its mother?

On her smellular device!

Kristin J. | Wausau, WI

So yesterday I was standing in the park and I was wondering why do Frisbees get so big when they get closer?

And then it hit me.

Sydney D. | Minnetonka, MN

What goes up and never comes down?

Your age.

Anonymous

You throw away the outside and cook the inside. Then, you eat the outside and throw away the inside. What did you eat?

Corn on the cob!

Kayla S. | Sunrise, FL

What do you call a bird that lives in a can?

A peli-can!

Anna E. | Surprise, AZ

Why did the student want to go to school in an airplane?

She wanted a higher education.

Callie B. | Rogersville, MO

How do you say "taco" in Spanish?

Taco!

Sophia P. | Irvine, CA

Why was the little strawberry so sad?

Because his parents were in a jam!

Cassidy T. | Minnetonka, MN

What is a mouse's favorite game?

Par-cheese-ee!

Grace F. | Agawam, MA

What do sea monsters like to eat?

Fish and ships.

Anonymous

What kind of bone will a dog not eat?

A trombone.

Evelyn C. | Clinton, NJ

Why did the turkey cross the road twice?

To prove he wasn't a chicken.

Charlie D. | Phoenix, AZ

What kind of music does a chiropractor listen to?

Hip hop!

Joseph T. | Saint Paul, MN

Where do cows like to travel in space?

The Milky Way.

Olivia S. | Naperville, IL

How does the man on the moon cut his hair?

Eclipse it! (He clips it!)

Makenna G. | Rochester, MN

Try saying this five times fast:

A tutor who tooted the flute, tried to tutor two tooters to toot. Said the two to the tutor, is it harder to toot or to tutor the tooters to toot?

Mylee B. | Oak Harbor, WA

What kind of horses play at night?

Night-mares.

Mackenzie T. | Saint Paul, MN

Why do birds fly south for the winter?

Because it's too far to walk!

Caleb W. | South Range, WI

How come cannibals don't eat clowns?

Because they taste funny!

Michael L. | Two Harbors, MN

UnitedHealthcare
Children's Foundation

What is a calculator's favorite food?

Pi.

Anonymous

Why are adults always asking little kids what they want to be when they grow up?

Because they are looking for ideas.

Aundrea R. | Little Chute, WI

What does a dog and a tree have in common?

Bark.

Luke E. | Illinois City, IL

Did you hear the one about the rope?

Skip it.

Shaelie S. | Brainerd, MN

What happens if you eat yeast and shoe polish for dinner?

You will rise and shine the next morning.

Anonymous

What do you call birds that are in love?

Lovebirds.

Alayna B. | Kronenwetter, WI

Why did the oven ask the toaster to marry him?

Because he got caught up in the heat of the moment.

Juldyz W. | Buffalo, MN

Which vegetables shave?

Carrots and cucumbers.

Catalina K. | Portland, CT

What do Alexander the Great and Kermit the Frog have in common?

The same middle name!

Jenna K. | Plymouth, MN

What do you get when you cross a snowman with a vampire?

Frost-bite.

Andrew N. | Hermitage, TN

What is the longest word in the English language?

"Smiles" because there is a mile between its first and last letters.

Daniele M. | Bloomington, MN

What do you call a grumpy cow?

MOO-dy!

Bryson S. | Booneville, MS

What kind of dance did the hamburgers go to?

A meat ball!

John H.　|　Lakeville, MN

What is a hyena's favorite candy?

A Snicker's bar.

Anonymous

Where does a crayon go on vacation?

Color-ado.

Aundrea R.　|　Little Chute, WI

What do you get when you cross Ebenezer Scrooge, a sheep and a fly that hums?

A BAAA-HUMbug.

Matthew E.　|　Maynard, MA

As two caterpillars were crawling along, a butterfly flew overhead. One turned to the other and said, "You'll never get me up in one of those things!"

Jake M. | Osseo, MN

Knock Knock.

Who's there?

(don't say anything)

Who's there?

Oh, sorry it's a secret. I can't tell you.

McKenzie A. | Acworth, GA

Why is 6 afraid of 7?

Because 7 8 9!

Glenn B. | Duluth, MN

What do you get from nervous cows?

Milk-shakes!

Chloe B. | Fleming Island, FL

What is a pirate's favorite letter?

Aye, ye may think it be the ARRRR, but it be the sea!

Aidan K. | Duluth, MN

Where do fish keep their money?

At the river bank!

Matthew K. | Coeur d'Alene, ID

What two things does a cow like best?

Milkshakes and MOO-sic!

Chayse B. | Rogersville, MO

Where does the snowman keep his money?

In the snow bank!

Cadyn E. | Lynd, MN

What did one plate say to the other plate?

Dinner's on me tonight!

Anonymous

Who do inches obey?

Their ruler.

Rhema S. | Springfield, MO

Who keeps the ocean clean?

The mermaid.

Gabi H. | La Porte, TX

What is a pretzel's favorite dance?

The Twist.

Rachel Q. | Apple Valley, MN

Do you know which president has the largest family?

George Washington, he is the nation's Founding Father.

Milana K. | Portland, CT

Where do french fries come from?

Greece.

Ronan T. | Shorewood, MN

What do you call a fish in a bow tie?

So-fish-ticated!

Meghan F. | Petal, MS

What did the hungry Dalmatian say after his meal?

That really hit the spot.

Emily S. | Rochester, MN

Why did the grape stop in the middle of the road?

Because it ran out of juice.

Anonymous

Why do Eskimos wash their clothes in Tide?

Because it's cold out-tide!

Avndrea R. | Little Chute, WI

I can't believe I got fired from the calendar factory. All I did was take a day off.

Ashton K. | Eden Prairie, MN

What seven letters are in an empty bottle?

O - I - C - U - R - M - T

Jenna N. | Eastvale, CA

What do you call a pig that plays basketball?

A ball hog!

Brianna M. | Mondovi, WI

Knock Knock.

Who's there?

Orange.

Orange who?

Orange you glad I didn't say banana?

Justin S. | Hyattsville, MD

What do you call a very popular perfume?

A best-smeller!

Isabel A. | Naperville, IL

UnitedHealthcare Children's Foundation

Why did the pirate go to the Caribbean?

He wanted some ARR & ARR!

Braden B. | Oak Harbor, WA

Where does a peacock go when it loses its tail?

A re-tail store!

Yszabehl S. | Neosho, MO

Why did the angry Jedi cross the road?

To get to the Dark Side!

Miles A. | Naperville, IL

Where does a 2,000 pound Gorilla sit?

Anywhere it wants to!

Shelby L. | Prior Lake, MN

Where do pirates shop?

Tarrrrrrget!

Gabby Y. | Duluth, MN

Why do golfers take an extra pair of socks?

In case they get a hole-in-one!

Miles A. | Naperville, IL

What kind of medicine do you put on a sick pig?

Oink-ment!

Darin M. | Weslaco, TX

If April showers bring May flowers, what do May flowers bring?

Pilgrims.

Anslee H. | Greensboro, NC

What is a Navy Seal's favorite color?

Aqua-Marine!

Ethan B. | Minneapolis, MN

What did the dog say to the cat?

I've got a bone to pick with you!

Benjamin T. | Thurman, NY

Jot down your own favorite jokes here!

YOU CAN BECOME ONE OF THE AUTHORS!

_____

_____

_____

_____

_____

_____

_____

_____

_____

UnitedHealthcare Children's Foundation

_____

_____

_____

_____

_____

_____

_____

_____

_____

_____

_____

_____

_____

_____

_____

_____

_____

_____

_____

_____

_____

_____

_____

_____

_____

_____

_____

_____

_____

_____

_____

_____

_____

_____

_____

_____

UnitedHealthcare
Children's Foundation

_____

_____

_____

_____

_____

_____

_____

_____

_____

_____

_____

_____

_____

_____

_____

_____

_____

_____

_____

_____

_____

_____

_____

_____

_____

_____

_____

_____

_____

_____

_____

_____

_____

_____

_____

_____

_____

_____

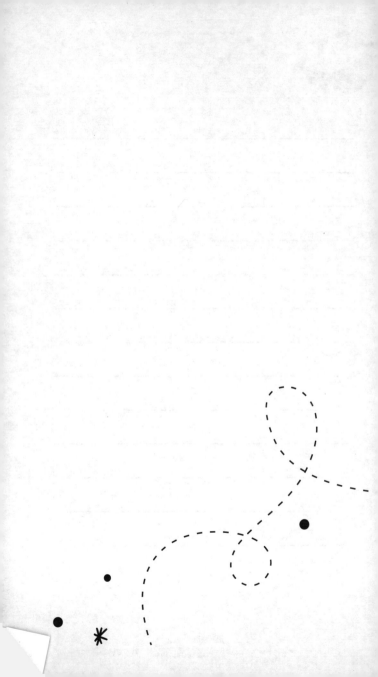